RUTH BADER GINSBURG

RUTH BADER GINSBURG

Iconic Supreme Court Justice

2ND EDITION

JAMES ROLAND

LERNER PUBLICATIONS ◆ MINNEAPOLIS

For my mother, Janette, an inspiration to all who know and love her

Lerner Publications Company
An imprint of Lerner Publishing Group, Inc.
241 First Avenue North
Minneapolis, MN 55401 USA

For reading levels and more information, look up this title at www.lernerbooks.com.

Image credits: AP Photo/Cliff Owen, p. 2; AP Photo/Doug Mills, p. 6; Collection of the Supreme Court of the United States, pp. 8, 9, 11, 14, 15, 19, 22, 24, 25, 26, 36, 41; AP Photo/Anthony Camerano, p. 10; Eustress/Wikimedia Commons (CC BY-SA 3.0), p. 13; Samir Luther/Flickr (CC BY-SA 2.0), p. 16; H. Armstrong Roberts/ClassicStock/Getty Images, p. 17; Library of Congress, p. 18; Beyond My Ken/Wikipedia Commons (CC BY-SA 4.0), p. 20; Bettmann/Getty Images, p. 23; David Hume Kennerly/Getty Images, pp. 27, 31; Ralph Alswang/William J. Clinton Library, p. 28; Fanny Carrier/AFP/Getty Images, p. 32; John Mottern/Stringer/Getty Images, p. 33; AP Photo/Stephen R. Brown, p. 35; Joanne Rathe/The Boston Globe/Getty Images, p. 38; Frazer Harrison/Getty Images, p. 39; Jess Pomponio/Shutterstock.com, p. 40.

Cover image: Chip Somodevilla/Getty Images.

Main body text set in Rotis Serif Std 55.
Typeface provided by Adobe Systems.

Editor: Andrea Nelson **Photo Editor:** Cynthia Zemlicka
Lerner team: Sue Marquis

Library of Congress Cataloging-in-Publication Data

Names: Roland, James, author.
Title: Ruth Bader Ginsburg : iconic Supreme Court justice / James Roland.
Description: 2nd edition. | Minneapolis, MN : Lerner Publications, [2021] | Series: Gateway biographies | Includes bibliographical references and index. | Audience: Ages 9–14 | Audience: Grades 4–6 | Summary: "In 1993 Ruth Bader Ginsburg became the second woman justice ever appointed to the US Supreme Court. Learn more about her life and career supporting gender equality and workers' rights"– Provided by publisher.
Identifiers: LCCN 2020000217 (print) | LCCN 2020000218 (ebook) | ISBN 9781541596764 (library binding) |ISBN 9781728400327 (ebook)
Subjects: LCSH: Ginsburg, Ruth Bader—Juvenile literature. | United States. Supreme Court—Biography—Juvenile literature. | Women judges—United States—Biography—Juvenile literature.
Classification: LCC KF8745.G56 R65 2021 (print) | LCC KF8745.G56 (ebook) | DDC 347.73/2634 [B]—dc23

LC record available at https://lccn.loc.gov/2020000217
LC ebook record available at https://lccn.loc.gov/2020000218

Manufactured in the United States of America
2-50603-48224-4/14/2021

CONTENTS

Ruth Bader Ginsburg walks with President Bill Clinton toward the White House Rose Garden on June 14, 1993.

On a sunny Sunday afternoon in June 1993, Ruth Bader Ginsburg stood quietly in the White House Rose Garden next to President Bill Clinton. US Supreme Court justice Byron White was retiring, and Clinton wanted Ginsburg to take White's place on the court. Ginsburg was excited about the opportunity. She would be just the second woman ever to serve on the Supreme Court. The first, Justice Sandra Day O'Connor, had been on the nation's highest court since 1981. During the Rose Garden ceremony introducing his selection to the public and the media, Clinton praised Ginsburg's distinguished career as a lawyer and then a judge. "Over the course of a lifetime, in her pioneering work on behalf of the women of this country, she has compiled a truly historic record of achievement in the finest traditions of American law and citizenship," he said.

When it was time to publicly accept the nomination, Ginsburg thanked Clinton and many others, including her husband, Martin. But she saved her last thank-you for her late mother. "I pray that I may be all that she would have been had she lived in an age when women could aspire and achieve, and daughters are cherished as much as sons," she said, as the president and others in attendance held back tears.

Ginsburg's mother, Celia Amster Bader, never attended college. Instead, she worked to help her family pay for her brother to get a college education. This was very common when she was young. Most women were not encouraged

In 1993 Ginsburg *(top right)* became the second woman to serve on the Supreme Court. The first woman was Sandra Day O'Connor *(bottom left)*.

to pursue college, let alone a career in law. But Celia Bader wanted her daughter to have more freedom and choices than she'd had. She set her daughter on a path that would make Ruth Bader Ginsburg an iconic figure in the American legal system and a role model for women and men alike.

Kiki

Ruth Bader was the second daughter of Celia and Nathan Bader. Her older sister, Marilyn, died of meningitis when Ruth was very young. Ruth, who was born in 1933, never had any other siblings. Nicknamed Kiki (pronounced "kicky") by her sister, Ruth was raised in the Flatbush area of Brooklyn, New York. Her father sold clothing, and her mother was a homemaker.

Ruth and her mother

Ruth went by the family nickname Kiki while growing up in the 1930s.

Brooklyn is one of five boroughs, or divisions, of New York City.

often visited the local library, fueling the future Supreme Court justice's passion for reading and knowledge. "One of my greatest pleasures as a child was sitting on my mother's lap when she would read to me, and then going to the library with her," Ruth said. "In fact, she deposited me in the children's section of the library and went to get her hair done. By the time she'd come back, I had the five books that I would take home for that week."

As an eighth grader, Ruth edited her school's student newspaper, the *Highway Herald*. She once wrote an editorial about some of the most important documents in history, including the Declaration of Independence and the United Nations charter. She was in her high school honor society.

Ruth twirled the baton on her high school's pep squad, the Go-Getters. As a member of the Go-Getters, she wore a black satin jacket, sold tickets to football games, and helped promote her school's sports teams in other ways. Ruth also loved music and played cello in the school orchestra. During the summers, Ruth attended Camp Che-Na-Wah, a Jewish summer camp in upstate New York. When she turned thirteen, she served as the camp rabbi, leading services for her fellow campers.

Before she had even reached her teen years, though, Ruth learned about discrimination against Jewish people. She and her family paid close attention to the Nazi persecution of Jews in Europe before and during World War II (1939–1945).

Even at home in the United States, life was sometimes difficult for

Ruth leads campers in prayer at Camp Che-Na-Wah in Minerva, New York, in 1948.

Jewish families. During one family trip in Pennsylvania, the Baders drove by a hotel sign that said, "No dogs or Jews allowed."

She would endure different types of discrimination later in life, especially as a woman in a field traditionally dominated by men. But these experiences helped shape Ruth's desire to help fight discrimination for the rest of her life.

Balancing Education and Family

In 1950 Ruth's mother died after a long battle with cancer. It was the day before Ruth was to graduate from Brooklyn's James Madison High School, a public school that currently includes a mock courtroom in its legal studies program named after the Supreme Court justice. Losing her mother was heartbreaking for Ruth. But she knew the best way to honor her mom's memory was to make the most of her education and career.

"My mother told me two things constantly," Bader recalled. "One was to be a lady, and the other was to be independent." And so young, independent Ruth Bader left Brooklyn for Cornell University in Ithaca, New York, determined to one day become a lawyer.

At Cornell Bader helped one of her professors with research on blacklists in the entertainment industry. In the United States in the 1950s, a blacklist was a list of people suspected of being Communists. People on these

Ginsburg studied government at Cornell University in Ithaca, New York, in the 1950s.

lists were sometimes fired from their jobs or were barred from getting work elsewhere. It didn't matter whether the person was truly a Communist or not. Once accused, that person's life was never the same.

Bader saw many attorneys risk their careers by defending blacklisted entertainers, college professors, and other individuals in court and before Congress. It wouldn't be long before Bader would be in court representing other people being treated unfairly. First, though, she would need to complete her schooling.

Bader graduated with honors with a bachelor of arts

degree in government. But the university was important to Bader in another lasting way. At Cornell she met Martin Ginsburg, a prelaw student. He was a year ahead of Bader in school. The two were college sweethearts who dated while Bader finished her last year at Cornell and Ginsburg started at Harvard Law School in Cambridge, Massachusetts.

They got married in June 1954, the same month Bader—now Ruth Bader Ginsburg—graduated at the top of her class from Cornell. But instead of going to Massachusetts with her husband, Ginsburg found

herself in Fort Sill, Oklahoma. Her husband was a US Army Reserve officer, and after Ginsburg's graduation, he was called up for active duty. In 1955 the couple had their first child, a daughter they named Jane.

After her husband's army duty ended, he returned to Harvard.

This portrait of Bader was taken in December 1953, during her senior year at Cornell.

Martin and Ruth were college sweethearts at Cornell. They were married on June 23, 1954.

Ginsburg also enrolled at Harvard Law School, but she wasn't able to focus entirely on her studies. She had to take care of baby Jane as well as Martin, who underwent surgery and treatment for testicular cancer the following year. But Ginsburg somehow managed to take care of everyone and everything at home while also becoming one of Harvard's top law students.

Ginsburg's experience at Harvard was difficult, though, and not just because of the demanding courses and the responsibilities at home. Women had been allowed to attend Harvard Law only since 1950. Just nine women were in Ginsburg's class of about five hundred first-year law students. The female students weren't given much respect. The dean even asked the women how they felt about taking away spots from qualified men.

Law students at Harvard face difficult classes and homework, but the program is known for producing some of the best lawyers in the world.

But Ginsburg persevered. She became the first woman on the *Harvard Law Review*. A law review is a journal with articles about court cases and other law-related subjects. The review is published by the best students at a law school. Ginsburg enjoyed writing. She later became one of the more prolific opinion writers on the Supreme Court. A court opinion is a summary of the case and an explanation of why the court ruled the way it did.

Despite her early academic success at Harvard, Ginsburg wouldn't get her degree there. Another big move was about to send her life in a new direction.

The Struggle to Find a Job

Martin Ginsburg had been offered a great job with a big law firm in New York City right after he graduated. The couple wanted to keep the family together in one place. Even though she was just a year from graduating, Ruth Bader Ginsburg left Harvard and transferred to Columbia Law School in New York. Both universities are part of a small group of schools that make up the prestigious Ivy League.

Ginsburg soon earned a place on the *Columbia Law Review*, becoming the first person ever to be part of the law reviews at both Harvard and Columbia. Ginsburg also graduated first in her class at Columbia. She faced less discrimination there compared with Harvard.

The Ginsburg family moved to New York City in 1958.

In spite of her glowing academic credentials, Ginsburg encountered some challenges in finding a job. Shortly after her Columbia graduation, Ginsburg was recommended by one of her professors to be a law clerk for Supreme Court justice Felix Frankfurter. Law clerks, sometimes called judicial clerks, help judges do research and write opinions on cases. It's a common entry-level position for new lawyers, and it helps recent graduates gain legal experience.

But Frankfurter, who had been on the Supreme Court since 1939, rejected Ginsburg. He said he wasn't ready to hire a woman. Ginsburg wasn't offered a job by any major

New York law firms either. As a woman and a mother, she faced a lot of discrimination. Ginsburg had worked for a summer for a large firm in New York. She had hoped that summer internship would turn into a job offer after graduation. Yet that offer never came.

Justice Felix Frankfurter served on the Supreme Court from January 1939 to August 1962.

Ginsburg and her husband play with their daughter, Jane, at home in New York in the summer of 1958.

But Ginsburg was not one to give up on her dreams. Many years later, Ginsburg told an interviewer that she could be grateful that she hadn't gotten the job with that New York law firm. She said sometimes in life a defeat can lead to a better opportunity later on.

"You think about what would have happened," Ginsburg said. "Suppose I had gotten a job as a permanent associate. Probably I would have climbed up the ladder and today I would be a retired partner. So often in life, things that you regard as an impediment turn out to be great good fortune."

Ginsburg finally got a job clerking for US district judge Edmund Palmieri in New York City. At the invitation of Columbia law professor Hans Smit, she left her clerk job after nearly two years to join Columbia's Project on International

Civil Procedure from 1961 to 1963. She researched laws and legal procedures from other countries and proposed ways that the legal system in the United States might be improved. As part of her work, Ginsburg learned Swedish and worked in Sweden briefly, helping a Swedish judge write a law book. She was later given an honorary degree from the University of Lund in Sweden.

The Columbia Project experience had a profound effect on the way Ginsburg approached her work as a judge and, later, as a Supreme Court justice. She often looked to international court cases to help her

In 1961 Ginsburg returned to Columbia University to work on the college's Project on International Civil Procedure.

form opinions on the cases she heard. This philosophy has earned her some criticism from people who think US judges should only interpret US cases and the Constitution to reach their decisions.

Smit tried to convince Columbia Law School to make Ginsburg a professor when the project ended. When that didn't work out, Ginsburg took a job as a law professor at Rutgers University Law School in New Jersey.

Fighting for Women's Rights

In 1965 the Ginsburgs had their second child, a son, James. Around that time, Ginsburg started her longtime involvement with women's rights. The New Jersey office of the American Civil Liberties Union (ACLU) was receiving frequent complaints of discrimination against women. The ACLU fights for individual rights and liberties under the laws of the United States. Many of the women's rights cases being handled by the New Jersey ACLU office found their way to Ginsburg at Rutgers.

The next several years were exciting, not just for Ginsburg but also for the women's movement. They were also very busy times. Ginsburg worked as both a law professor and an attorney helping the ACLU with many cases. One discrimination case went all the way to the Supreme Court in 1971. The justices ruled in favor of Ginsburg's side. A year later, the ACLU created the Women's Rights Project. Ginsburg was named codirector.

Also in 1972, Ginsburg accepted a job offer from Columbia Law School, making her the first tenured woman on its faculty. Tenured college professors cannot be fired unless the college proves that they did something wrong.

The 1970s saw many changes for women in the United States. A wider variety of careers were opening up to women, and the number of women graduating from college rose dramatically. But a lot of laws were unfair to women. And in many parts of the country, women were still fighting for equal treatment and equal opportunities. In the middle of that fight was Ginsburg. She believed very strongly that men and women shouldn't be treated differently under the law. She bravely took on cases aimed at erasing those differences in state and national laws.

From 1973 to 1976, she argued six women's rights cases before the Supreme Court and won five of them.

This work, along with other cases she took on in lower courts, helped women make great strides in achieving legal equality.

The first case she argued and won before the Supreme Court, *Frontiero v. Richardson*, was in 1973. A female air force lieutenant, Sharron Frontiero, and her husband, Joseph Frontiero, challenged a law that treated male and female military service members differently. Under the law, a man in the armed services could claim his wife as a legal dependent and qualify for an increased housing allowance, even if his wife did not depend on his income. But a married woman in the service had to prove that she provided her husband with more than half his financial support for her to qualify for the extra allowance. Ginsburg argued that such laws were prejudiced against women. She successfully proved

Joseph and Sharron Frontiero sued the US Department of Defense for gender discrimination. Ginsburg argued the Frontiero case before the Supreme Court in 1973.

Ginsburg with her daughter, Jane, and son, James, in December 1979

that there was no reason for the law to treat men and women differently.

In another case, *Duren v. Missouri*, she argued that a Missouri law was unfair because it said that men had to sit on juries but that women had the option not to serve on jury duty. Ginsburg believed this law was basically saying that women weren't as important as men in the court system. The court agreed, and she won the case.

After spending most of the 1970s as an attorney arguing cases before judges, Ginsburg would spend the rest of her career listening to arguments and ruling on cases. But her role in the fight for women's rights and greater equality for everyone would only grow in the years ahead.

Appointed Judge and Justice

During the administration of President Jimmy Carter (1977–1981), the Supreme Court had no openings. But Carter did nominate many people as judges on federal courts around the nation. There are several types of federal courts. They hear cases involving the constitutionality of a law, disputes between states, international treaties, and other major issues. Federal courts have authority over state and local courts, though not as much power as the Supreme Court.

Carter made a special effort to nominate more women and minorities as judges in these important courts. In 1980, shortly before he lost his reelection bid to Ronald Reagan, Carter named Ginsburg to the US Court of Appeals in Washington, DC. Thirteen federal courts of appeals operate around the country. They are one step below the Supreme Court in the US legal system. A court of appeals has a panel of three judges

Ginsburg in her judicial robes during her first term on the US Court of Appeals in 1980

instead of a jury to decide each case. If someone loses in a US Court of Appeals, the next and final stop is the Supreme Court.

While on the US Court of Appeals in Washington, DC, Ginsburg wrote more than three hundred opinions. She also developed a reputation for building consensus among her fellow panel judges. Among the judges she served with was Antonin Scalia. Despite their contrasting political and judicial philosophies, Scalia and Ginsburg became friends. Scalia was appointed to the Supreme Court in 1986 and continued his friendly sparring with Ginsburg when she joined him seven years later.

By the time Scalia was named to the Supreme Court, Sandra Day O'Connor was already a justice. So the idea that Ginsburg might one day make it to the Supreme Court wasn't too outrageous. In 1981 Reagan selected O'Connor as the first female Supreme Court justice. Even though O'Connor was considered a conservative judge and Ginsburg a liberal judge, Ginsburg was thrilled

Antonin Scalia served with Ginsburg on both the US Court of Appeals and the Supreme Court. The two justices were close friends.

that a woman was finally part of the highest court in the nation.

"I thought it was terrific for the country," Ginsburg said later. "There was no chance that I was going to be nominated by President Reagan. But it was certainly time. I remember being in my car, turning on the radio, hearing the news, and thinking, 'Isn't this grand!'"

After O'Connor, the next four Supreme Court justices to be appointed were Scalia, Anthony Kennedy, David Souter, and Clarence Thomas. Then, in June 1993, only a few months after being sworn into office, Clinton made his first appointment to the high court. He named Ginsburg, making her the second female justice and the first Jewish female justice. The second Jewish woman to serve on the Supreme Court was Justice Elena Kagan. She was appointed by President Barack Obama in 2010, four years after Sandra Day O'Connor retired. The previous year, Obama had appointed Justice Sonia Sotomayor to the high court. For about two hundred years, no women had been on the Supreme

Court. By the fall of 2010, three of the nine justices were women.

During her first week on the Supreme Court, Ginsburg wasted little time in establishing herself as an enthusiastic justice. She dove right into her first case, questioning the lawyers who were presenting it.

At a 2015 event at Harvard, retired Justice David Souter introduced Ginsburg by sharing his initial impression of her. Souter and Scalia were known to be aggressive questioners of attorneys during Supreme Court

Ginsburg takes the oath of office on August 10, 1993, while her husband, Martin (*center*), looks on.

cases. But Ginsburg started firing off questions before anyone else could speak. Souter told the crowd at Harvard that Scalia whispered to him, "You and I may have asked our last question in this courtroom." Souter also referred to Ginsburg as a "tiger justice."

Role in the Supreme Court

Though assertive in the courtroom, Ginsburg had a reputation for encouraging friendliness among her fellow justices. She and Scalia often had very different opinions on cases and were frequently vocal in their disagreements. However, they were good friends for many years. They attended the opera together and even vacationed together. Before Ginsburg's husband died in 2010, the Ginsburgs always had New Year's Eve dinner with Scalia and his wife, Maureen Scalia.

In a 2015 *Time* magazine article that named Ginsburg one of the 100 Most Influential People, Justice Scalia complimented his dear friend for her intelligence and her positive influence on the other eight justices. He wrote, "I can attest that her opinions are always thoroughly considered, always carefully crafted, and almost always correct (which is to say we sometimes disagree) . . . her suggestions improve the opinions the rest of us write."

When Scalia died suddenly in 2016, Ginsburg remembered him fondly. "He was a jurist of captivating brilliance and wit," she said, and called him a "treasured friend."

THE SUPREME COURT

The Supreme Court is made up of nine justices. When there is an opening on the court, the president nominates a judge to fill it. The US Senate must approve the nomination before the judge can be sworn in as a Supreme Court justice. Members of the Supreme Court are referred to as justices, to distinguish them from other judges.

The cases that come before the Supreme Court usually have national importance and involve very serious subjects. These cases have been argued and appealed in lower courts. The Supreme Court's job is to interpret the Constitution to help reach a decision. The Supreme Court can also decide whether federal, state, and even local governments are acting constitutionally. And the Constitution gives the Supreme Court the power to decide whether the president is acting within the law.

Justices listen to lawyers representing both sides and ask questions to better understand the case. Justices meet by themselves, without an audience or the media present, to discuss the case. The justices also do a lot of reading. They study the background of the case they are hearing, as well as similar cases. The justices finally vote on the case. Sometimes, it is a unanimous vote, 9–0. But it can often be a close 5–4 vote. The decisions are final and cannot be appealed. If the vote isn't unanimous, one justice writes the majority opinion and a justice in the minority writes the dissenting opinion. These opinions are entered into the official record of the Supreme Court for the public to read.

Ginsburg also enjoyed a close relationship with O'Connor, who retired from the Supreme Court in 2006. "She has been very much like a big sister," Ginsburg said of O'Connor. "I think we have an enormous affection and respect for each other, even though on some very important issues we are going to be on opposite sides."

On some cases, Ginsburg and O'Connor were very much in agreement. In 1996 Ginsburg and the other justices ruled on a case that in many ways summed up her longtime fight for equal rights for women. In *United States v. Virginia*, the Supreme Court ruled that the Virginia Military Institute (VMI) should have to admit women. For more than 150 years, VMI had trained men to become army officers. Ginsburg wrote the opinion for the majority, which included O'Connor, that women should have the same opportunities as men, including the right to attend a public university such as VMI.

In many cases, however, Ginsburg faced opposition from

Ginsburg sits in her chambers at the Supreme Court in Washington, DC, in 2002.

Lilly Ledbetter filed a lawsuit in 1998 over gender-based pay discrimination at her workplace.

the majority of justices. In one well-known case, *Ledbetter v. Goodyear Tire & Rubber Co.*, Ginsburg was in the minority of a 5–4 vote. But even though the vote didn't go Ginsburg's way, the case eventually led to a change in federal law that benefited women in the workplace.

In the case, a Goodyear manager named Lilly Ledbetter complained that her salary was consistently less than male managers doing similar work, even though the men had the same amount of experience as Ledbetter or even less. The case was complicated. The key issue involved the amount of time an employee has to file a charge of pay discrimination. Ledbetter hadn't made her complaint within the required 180 days of Goodyear's decision not to increase her salary. But her case would lead to a change in the way companies had to respond to such complaints. Two years after the case was decided, Obama signed into law the Lilly Ledbetter Fair Pay Act of 2009. It changed the way the 180-day rule is applied, making it easier for employees to challenge the fairness of their pay.

In one of the most controversial cases to come before the Supreme Court during Ginsburg's time on the bench, she was again in the minority. The case was *Bush v. Gore*, and it determined the outcome of the 2000 presidential election. The case centered on a dispute between the candidates, Vice President Al Gore and Texas governor George W. Bush, about the vote totals and recount procedures in Florida. The justices voted 5–4 that the Florida Supreme Court had acted unconstitutionally in the way it ruled on the recount. The decision essentially sealed the victory for Bush.

Even though Ginsburg was in the minority, the case did underscore her belief that the Supreme Court should, at times, defer to other levels of government. In this famous case, she believed that the United States Supreme Court should not have overruled the Florida Supreme Court's decision in how a state law was being interpreted. She argued that the matter of recount deadlines and other procedures were the responsibility of Florida officials or perhaps Congress, and not the United States Supreme Court.

Al Gore (*left*) and George W. Bush were candidates in the 2000 presidential election. The results were so close that the state of Florida had to recount its ballots to confirm an accurate tally.

Every Supreme Court justice is in the majority or the minority at some point. Ginsburg once said that it does bother her when the votes don't go her way. But she doesn't stay down for long. "I'm dejected, but only momentarily, when I can't get the fifth vote for something I think is very important," she said. "But then you go on to the next challenge and you give it your all. You know that these important issues are not going to go away. They are going to come back again and again. There'll be another time, another day."

Away from Court

Though being a judge is a time-consuming job, Ginsburg always found time for her other interests. She loved reading, especially mystery stories. Her favorite authors were Amanda Cross and Dorothy Sayers.

Ginsburg also loved music, especially opera. Her favorite composers include Verdi, Puccini, and Mozart. Because the Washington, DC, opera community knew about Ginsburg's love of opera, she was invited to be part of two productions in the nation's capital. In a Washington National Opera production of *Ariadne auf Naxos*, she was an extra wearing full makeup and a powdered wig. She was joined onstage by fellow justice Scalia, also a big opera fan.

In another production, a famous lighthearted operetta called *Die Fledermaus*, she appeared as herself. Two

Ginsburg (*center*) appeared in a production of the opera *Ariadne auf Naxos* in January 1994. Justice Scalia (*center right*) joined her in the performance.

other justices, Stephen Breyer and Anthony Kennedy, also appeared with Ginsburg. All three wore their black justice robes and played party guests. Ginsburg dressed up her costume with a colorful fan. She has a reputation for accessorizing her judicial robes with fancy neckwear called jabots. A jabot is usually made of lace and hangs from the neck over a shirt or, in Ginsburg's case, over a Supreme Court justice robe.

For most of her life, Ginsburg attended concerts, operas, and other events with her devoted husband, Martin. He too had a distinguished career as an attorney. Later in his life, he was a professor at Georgetown University Law Center in Washington, DC. The Ginsburgs

celebrated their fifty-sixth wedding anniversary shortly before Martin died in 2010.

Ginsburg remained close to her children and her four grandchildren, though they lived in different cities. Jane Ginsburg, the older of her children, is a law professor at Columbia University, the same school from which her famous mother earned her law degree in 1954 and later worked as a professor. James Ginsburg shares his mother's longtime love of music. He is a classical music producer in Chicago.

Along with being an inspiration to her children and countless other people around the world, Ginsburg is also a survivor. In late 2018 Ginsburg fell in her office and broke three ribs. During the summer of 2019, she was treated for cancer. A month later, she voiced her plans to remain on the bench. Ginsburg also had been treated for cancer in 1999, 2009, and 2018.

Undeterred by these health challenges and her advancing age, Ginsburg remained an energetic member of the Supreme Court, a guest speaker at university graduations and other events, and an involved grandmother. In 2016, at the age of eighty-three, she made it clear that she had no intentions of stepping down from her position, despite pressure from those who thought she was getting too old for the job.

"I will retire when it's time," Ginsburg said. "And, when is it time? When I can't do the job full-steam."

Icon of History and Pop Culture

Ginsburg has been a pioneer. When she started at Harvard Law, only about 3 percent of the students were women. In 2020 about half of Harvard's law students were women. As an attorney, she helped change laws that ended many types of discrimination, especially against women. And as a judge and later a Supreme Court justice, she continued to work toward a fairer society. "I try to teach through my opinions, through my speeches, how wrong it is to judge people on the basis of what they look like, color of their skin, whether they're men or women," she said.

In 2015 Ginsburg received a medal from Harvard's Radcliffe Institute for Advanced Study for her exceptional legal career and societal impact. At the ceremony, Radcliffe dean Lizabeth Cohen noted Ginsburg's role in creating opportunities for women: "We are here today to honor how one person—our honoree, Ruth Bader Ginsburg—knocked on closed doors, opened them, and held them open for others."

Ginsburg speaks onstage about her inspiring career after receiving the 2015 Radcliffe Medal.

When it was her turn to speak, Ginsburg urged young women to continue knocking. "Fight for the things that you care about," she said. "But do it in a way that will lead others to join you."

A lifetime of fighting for fair play has earned Ginsburg individual accolades and honors. But Ginsburg insisted that she and the other justices place the importance of the Supreme Court above any personal goals or achievements.

While Ginsburg's legal career cemented her place in American history, it also made her something of a pop culture icon. In 2015 *Scalia/Ginsburg,* a comic opera based on the conflicting legal opinions and arguments between the two justices, had its world premiere. That same year, *Saturday Night Live* cast member Kate McKinnon began playing Ginsburg as a recurring character. And a Tumblr blog dubbed the justice Notorious RBG, referencing the late rapper and fellow Brooklyn native Notorious B.I.G.

Ginsburg published a book, *My Own Words*, a collection of her writings that became a *New York Times* best seller. She also maintained an incredible workout routine that had her performing push-ups and planks, lifting weights, and tossing medicine balls. It kept her healthy and fit—and not just for a woman her age. In fact, a much younger reporter who tried it wrote an article about his grueling experience headlined "I Did Ruth Bader Ginsburg's Workout. It Nearly Broke Me."

Ginsburg, however, was always eager to get in the gym, even when it meant leaving the work she was so passionate about. "When it comes time to meet my trainer, I drop everything," she said.

Whether they admired her determination, drive, judicial perspective, or physical strength, people just couldn't get enough of Ginsburg. In 2018 she was the subject of two movies, a documentary, *RBG,* and a

feature film, *On the Basis of Sex.* Fans of the Supreme Court justice bought Notorious RBG mugs and Ruth Bader Ginsburg action figures. They wore clothes emblazoned with her face and carried bags printed with her words: "Women belong in all places where decisions are being made."

A fan shows off a Ruth Bader Ginsburg action figure.

A protester holds a sign bearing Ginsburg's likeness during the 2019 Women's March.

For her part, Ginsburg took it all in stride, keeping her focus on her work and her desire to make society better. When asked how she'd like to be remembered, Ginsburg didn't mention the fame or all her accomplishments and all the barriers she helped knock down. Instead, in her usual humble manner, she said she hoped people would think of her as "someone who used whatever talent she had to do her work to the very best of her ability. And to help repair tears in her society, to make things a little better through the use of whatever ability she has."

In December of 2019, Ginsburg accepted the Berggruen Prize, an award given to a significant individual in the field of philosophy. The prize committee chose Ginsburg for the prize from more than five hundred nominees.

"Few in our era have done more to bring vital philosophical ideas to fruition in practical affairs than Ruth Bader Ginsburg," said philosopher Kwame Anthony Appiah, chairman of the Berggruen Prize committee and a professor at New York University.

On September 18, 2020, Ginsburg died at her home in Washington, DC, surrounded by her family. She was eighty-seven. Ginsburg served on the Supreme Court for twenty-seven years, becoming one of its most iconic members.

"Our nation has lost a jurist of historic stature," Chief Justice John Roberts said in a statement from the Supreme Court. "Today we mourn, but with confidence that future generations will remember Ruth Bader Ginsburg as we knew her—a tireless and resolute champion of justice."

Former President Bill Clinton, who nominated Ginsburg to the Supreme Court, said that the justice had exceeded the expectations he had when he nominated her in 1993. "Her landmark opinions advancing gender equality,

marriage equality, the rights of people with disabilities, the rights of immigrants, and so many more moved us closer to 'a more perfect union,'" he said.

Ginsburg stands with fellow Supreme Court justices Sonia Sotomayor (*left*) and Elena Kagan.

IMPORTANT DATES

1933   Ruth Bader Ginsburg is born on March 15 in Brooklyn, New York.

1954   She graduates first in her class from Cornell University in June. A few weeks later, she marries Martin Ginsburg.

1955   She gives birth to her first child, Jane, on July 21.

1956   She enrolls in Harvard Law School and eventually becomes the first woman on the *Harvard Law Review.*

1958   She transfers to Columbia Law School and serves on the *Columbia Law Review.*

1959   She earns her law degree from Columbia, finishing at the top of her class.

1963   She starts teaching at Rutgers Law School.

1965   She gives birth to her second child, James.

1972   She becomes codirector of the ACLU's Women's Rights Project. She also becomes the first woman to be a tenured professor at Columbia Law School.

1980	President Carter names Ginsburg to the US Court of Appeals in Washington, DC.
1993	President Clinton nominates Ginsburg to the Supreme Court. She is sworn in that fall.
1999	She is treated for cancer and recovers.
2007	Ginsburg writes the dissenting opinion in *Ledbetter v. Goodyear Tire & Rubber Co.*, which led Congress to enact the Lilly Ledbetter Fair Pay Act two years later.
2009	She receives treatment for cancer and recovers again.
2010	Her husband, Martin, dies soon after the Ginsburgs' fifty-sixth wedding anniversary.
2018	Two films about her life, *RBG* and *On the Basis of Sex*, are released.
2019	She is awarded the Berggruen Prize.
2020	She dies at home at the age of eighty-seven on September 18.

SOURCE NOTES

7   William J. Clinton, "Remarks Announcing the Nomination of Ruth
     Bader Ginsburg to Be a Supreme Court Associate Justice," American
     Presidency Project, June 14, 1993, https://www.presidency.ucsb.edu
     /documents/remarks-announcing-the-nomination-ruth-bader-ginsburg
     -be-supreme-court-associate-justice.

8   Ruth Bader Ginsburg, quoted in Richard L. Berke, "The Supreme Court:
     The Overview; Clinton Names Ruth Ginsburg, Advocate for Women,
     to Court," *New York Times*, June 15, 1993, http://www.nytimes
     .com/1993/06/15/us/supreme-court-overview-clinton-names-ruth
     -ginsburg-advocate-for-women-court.html.

10   Ruth Bader Ginsburg, quoted in Nadine Epstein, "Ruth Bader Ginsburg:
     'The Notorious RBG,'" *Moment*, May/June 2015, http://www.momentmag
     .com/ruth-bader-ginsburg-notorious-rbg-interview/.

12   Malvina Halberstam, "Ruth Bader Ginsburg," Jewish Women's Archive,
     accessed March 1, 2009, http://jwa.org/encyclopedia/article/ginsburg
     -ruth-bader.

12   Ruth Bader Ginsburg, quoted in Sandra Pullman, "Tribute: The Legacy
     of Ruth Bader Ginsburg and WRP Staff," ACLU, accessed July 27, 2015,
     https://www.aclu.org/tribute-legacy-ruth-bader-ginsburg-and-wrp-staff.

19   "Ruth Bader Ginsburg: Legal Pioneer," Makers, accessed August 19,
     2015, https://www.yahoo.com/lifestyle/ruth-bader-ginsburg-legal
     -pioneer-013635291.html.

27   Ruth Bader Ginsburg, quoted in "A Conversation with Justice Ruth
     Bader Ginsburg," *Record* 56, no. 1 (Winter 2001), http://www2.nycbar
     .org/Publications/record/winter01.1.pdf.

29   Antonin Scalia, quoted in Colleen Walsh, "Honoring Ruth Bader
     Ginsburg," *Harvard Gazette*, May 29, 2015, http://news.harvard.edu
     /gazette/story/2015/05/honoring-ruth-bader-ginsburg/.

29   David Souter, quoted in Walsh.

29   Antonin Scalia, "Ruth Bader Ginsburg," *Time*, April 16, 2015, http://
     time.com/3823889/ruth-bader-ginsburg-2015-time-100/.

29   Ginsburg, quoted in Brett LoGiurato, "Ruth Bader Ginsburg Released a Moving Tribute to Her 'Best Buddy,' Antonin Scalia," Business Insider, February 14, 2016, https://www.businessinsider.com/ruth-bader-ginsburg-scalia-death-2016-2.

31   Ginsburg, quoted in "A Conversation with Justice Ruth Bader Ginsburg."

34   Ginsburg, quoted in "A Conversation with Justice Ruth Bader Ginsburg."

37   Nina Totenberg, "No, Ruth Bader Ginsburg Does Not Intend to Retire Anytime Soon," NPR, October 3, 2016, https://www.npr.org/2016/10/03/495820477/no-ruth-bader-ginsburg-does-not-intend-to-retire-anytime-soon.

37   Ruth Bader Ginsburg, quoted in Irin Carmon, "Exclusive Justice Ruth Bader Ginsburg Interview," MSNBC, February 17, 2015, http://www.msnbc.com/msnbc/exclusive-justice-ruth-bader-ginsburg-interview-full-transcript.

37   Lizabeth Cohen, quoted in Walsh, "Honoring Ruth Bader Ginsburg."

38   Ginsburg, quoted in Walsh.

39   "*The David Rubenstein Show*: Ruth Bader Ginsburg," Bloomberg, October 2, 2019, https://www.bloomberg.com/news/videos/2019-10-02/the-david-rubenstein-show-ruth-bader-ginsburg-video.

39   Bill Mears, "Justice Ginsburg Ready to Welcome Sotomayor," CNN, accessed October 2, 2019, https://www.cnn.com/2009/POLITICS/06/16/sotomayor.ginsburg/index.html.

40   Ginsburg, quoted in Carmon, "Exclusive Ginsburg Interview."

40   Kwame Anthony Appiah, quoted in Jennifer Schuessler, "Ruth Bader Ginsburg Wins $1 Million Berggruen Prize," *New York Times*, October 23, 2019, https://www.nytimes.com/2019/10/23/arts/ruth-bader-ginsburg-berggruen-prize.html.

41   John Roberts, "Statements from the Supreme Court Regarding the Death of Associate Justice Ruth Bader Ginsburg," news release no. 09-19-20, September 19, 2020, https://www.supremecourt.gov/publicinfo/press/pressreleases/pr_09-19-20.

41   Bill Clinton, "Statement from President Clinton on the Passing of Justice Ruth Bader Ginsburg," Clinton Foundation, September 18, 2020, https://www.clintonfoundation.org/press-releases/statement-president-clinton-passing-justice-ruth-bader-ginsburg-0.

SELECTED BIBLIOGRAPHY

Burton, Danielle. "10 Things You Didn't Know about Ruth Bader Ginsburg."
U.S. News and World Report, October 1, 2007. http://www.usnews.com
/news/national/articles/2007/10/01/10-things-you-didnt-know-about-ruth
-bader-ginsburg.

Craig, Jon. "Ruth Bader Ginsburg Reminisces about Her Time on the Hill."
Cornell Chronicle, September 22, 2014. http://www.news.cornell.edu
/stories/2014/09/ruth-bader-ginsburg-reminisces-about-her-time-hill.

Halberstam, Malvina. "Ruth Bader Ginsburg." Jewish Women's Archive, March 1,
2009. http://jwa.org/encyclopedia/article/ginsburg-ruth-bader.

Pullman, Sandra. "Tribute: The Legacy of Ruth Bader Ginsburg and WRP Staff."
ACLU. Accessed July 27, 2015. https://www.aclu.org/tribute-legacy-ruth
-bader-ginsburg-and-wrp-staff.

Walsh, Colleen. "Honoring Ruth Bader Ginsburg." *Harvard Gazette*, May 29,
2015. http://news.harvard.edu/gazette/story/2015/05/honoring-ruth-bader
-ginsburg/.

FURTHER READING

BOOKS

Ahrens, Niki. *Sonia Sotomayor: First Latina Supreme Court Justice.*
Minneapolis: Lerner Publications, 2021.
Read about Sonia Sotomayor, who grew up in a working-class family and
eventually became a lawyer and Supreme Court justice.

Demuth, Patricia Brennan. *Who Is Ruth Bader Ginsburg?* New York: Penguin
Workshop, 2019.
Learn more about Ruth Bader Ginsburg and what makes her an iconic figure.

Sonneborn, Liz. *The Supreme Court: Why It Matters to You.* New York:
Children's Press, 2020.
Discover how Supreme Court justices can change the course of US history.

WEBSITES

How Do US Supreme Court Justices Get Appointed?
https://thekidshouldseethis.com/post/supreme-court-justices-how-appointed
-ted-ed
Discover what it takes to be appointed to the US Supreme Court.

Interactive Constitution
http://constitutioncenter.org/interactive-constitution
Learn more about this key document of the United States, which Supreme
Court justices work to uphold.

Supreme Court of the United States
http://www.supremecourt.gov
At the official Supreme Court website, you can read about cases the justices
are hearing and those that will soon go before the court. You can also read
official opinions by the justices and learn more about the court.

INDEX